GOD THINGS
COME IN SMALL
PACKAGES

for WOMEN

*Susan Duke, Judy Carden,
and LeAnn Weiss*

To schedule author appearances, write: Author Appearances, Starburst Promotions, P.O. Box 4123, Lancaster, Pennsylvania 17604 or call (717) 293-0939. Website: www.starburstpublishers.com.

CREDITS:
Cover design by Richmond & Williams
Text design by Steve Diggs and Friends, Nashville

All Scripture was taken from the HOLY BIBLE: NEW INTERNA-TIONAL VERSION® NIV®. Copyright© 1973, 1978, 1984 by International Bible Society.

First Printing, October 2000
ISBN: 1-892016-35-4
Library of Congress Catalog Number 00-101393
Printed in USA

Contents

INTRODUCTION

By Susan Duke

Woman must be the pioneer in this turning inward for strength. In a sense she has always been the pioneer. —**Anne Morrow Lindbergh**

As sojourners in this life, women share a unique bond—a bond that transcends age, race, and status. Through the ages, women have been called mysterious, intuitive, nurturing, resourceful, relational, tender, and emotional. And indeed, we are all of these—but, as daughters of heaven, when we celebrate and unwrap our God-given gifts, we joyfully find our place and calling within a world that needs us.

Throughout our journey, women are entrusted with special privileges—creating homes, tending hearts, planting hopes, harvesting dreams, and embracing the generous joys of being all God has created us to be.

Somehow I think God must have known women would celebrate our differences fervently, freely, and joyously—savoring the moments that set us apart.

May the stories from our hearts shine a beacon of light upon your hearts, help you discover and unearth new dimensions in your soul, and inspire you to celebrate being a woman!

I praise you because I am fearfully and wonderfully made.
—Psalm 139:14

*R*emember days that have passed and consider your generational heritage. I'm able to surpass even your biggest dreams because of My power, which is working in your life. All things are possible with Me!

Creatively,

Your Awesome God

———————— ⬦ ————————

Deuteronomy 32:7; Ephesians 3:20; Mark 10:27

ONCE UPON A MEMORY

By Judy Carden

$\mathcal{J}$t had been the perfect day at Disney World.

From the get-go, six-year-old Aubrey had pretty much directed the itinerary for our trio of grandmother, daughter, and granddaughter. Throughout the day her sparkling eyes and checkerboard grin proved that magic existed.

"Do we really have to leave?" Aubrey asked.

If only I could have suspended time in this magic kingdom, but the park was about to close. As it was, as the lingering swirls of color disappeared from the evening sky, I led our trio toward the tram that would transport us back to reality.

"Mommy, can we go to Cinderella's castle one more time?" Aubrey pleaded, tugging me by my sleeve. "Maybe we'll see Cinderella again, or maybe her fairy godmother," she pressed, her eyes growing wide with wonder.

How do you say "no" to a six-year-old who still believes in fairy godmothers?

So the three of us, strolling hand in hand, wound around the sidewalks until we reached the shimmering towers of Cinderella's castle, illuminated by the twinkling of a billion starry lights. There we stood—three generations of women—our hearts holding on to the remnants of a day we wished would last a lifetime.

Staring at the castle but speaking to my mother, Aubrey said, "Grandma Fry, I don't ever want to forget today."

Not missing a beat, Mother answered, "Then close your eyes and take a picture with your heart. And when tomorrow has come and gone, and you want to remember today, pull the picture from your heart."

"The magic too, Grandma?" whispered Aubrey.

"The magic too," Mother whispered back, clasping her fingers around Aubrey's outstretched hand.

Two decades later, three generations of women still remember the magic.

We needn't always travel far and wide

to feel the wonder and magic of life.

When we wish to relive those

"fairytale" moments, our hearts

need only rewind to the reel that's

titled "Once upon a Memory."

$\mathcal{F}$aith is seeing and acting with My eyes. Don't be afraid of stepping out of your comfort zone, just believe in Me! I constantly watch your comings and goings. Wherever you go, you can count on My divine guidance. My right hand securely holds you. Remember, I'm for you! No obstacle is too difficult with Me on your side. When you seek Me first, I'll open incredible doors for you.

Faithfully,

God

———————————— ✶ ————————————

Hebrews 11:1; Mark 5:36; Psalms 121:8; 139:9–10;
Romans 8:31; Jeremiah 32:27; Matthew 6:33

WINGS OF FAITH

By Susan Duke

One afternoon a few years ago, my husband arrived home from work to find me red-eyed and looking pathetic. Tenderly, he put his arms around me and asked, "What's wrong, Honey? Has something happened?"

"Yeah," I blubbered, "something's happened, alright. I've gotten myself into something I'll never be able to do—writing my first book!"

"Honey," he said gently, "God is giving you a wonderful opportunity. You can do it." His words didn't console me.

The next morning, I poured myself a cup of coffee, gathered my Bible and a devotional book, and shuffled out the back door for some quiet time on the deck. Sitting at our patio table, I clutched my coffee cup and held it close, letting the hot steam warm my face. I closed my eyes and listened.

A cool breeze swept over me, awakening me to the freshness of the morning. The birds were singing cheerfully while gathering twigs and leaves for nest building.

I was reminded of a story I'd heard about baby birds learning to fly. The mama bird combines twigs, soft feathers, and other materials to make a comfortable nest for her newly hatched babies. Then, as her baby birds grow, the mama bird inserts more prickly twigs and small limbs into the nest, making the now-crowded nest uncomfortable—subtly preparing her babies for graduation day—when she nudges them out of the nest and forces them to fly.

I remembered another spring day when I observed a baby bird that fell to the ground. I marveled at the quick response of the mama bird as she swooped down and gently lifted the baby, coaxing the flapping of its tiny wings to action. I could almost hear her saying, "Come on, you can do it! This is what you were created for—to fly! I believe in you! You must believe too!"

That morning, I felt that God was gently whispering to me, *"Do you want to stay in your comfortable nest—or do you believe you can fly?"*

Despite growing pains and sharp twinges of discomfort . . . I knew.

It was graduation day.

Standing up, I lifted my face heavenward and held out my arms—flapping invisible wings of faith—and answered, "Yes, Lord, I believe I can fly!"

It's much easier staying in our comfort

zone than taking a leap of faith. But

God is ever nudging us to trust him

and believe he will help us soar to

new horizons.

I am so close to you when you're brokenhearted. I personally comfort you. Whether you live or die, you belong to Me. I'll wipe away every tear from your eyes, leading you to springs of Living Water. My plans stand firm and the purposes of My heart continue through all generations. My goodness and mercy will follow you all of the days of your life, and you'll dwell in My house forever.

I've Gone to Prepare a

Place for You,

Your Heavenly Father

———————— ⬤ ————————

Psalm 34:18; Isaiah 51:12; Romans 14:8; Revelation 7:17; Psalm 33:11; Psalm 23:6; John 14:3

TRIBUTE TO A PRINCESS

By LeAnn Weiss

"LeAnn, quick turn on the TV," my sister yelled.

News of Princess Diana's tragic accident had just hit the air, and we stayed up all night crying as we watched.

Details of her fatal car crash caused me to think back twenty-five years to the weekend just before I started first grade. After waiting several hours for Mommy to come home from a women's retreat, my dad rushed off when he received the call that our churchwomen had been in an accident. My siblings and I fell asleep waiting for my parents to come home.

Early the next morning, Dad seated us on the living room couch. "Daddy, when's Mommy getting up for church?" we quizzed.

He tearfully told us that Mommy was in heaven. A truck had skidded in the rain, instantly killing Mom and another friend and seriously injuring others.

Twenty-five years later, watching the continuous coverage of Princess Diana's death brought back so many memories of my mom, who was only thirty-four at the time of her tragic death.

A timely e-mail from my dad addressing the twenty-fifth anniversary of my mom's death comforted me. Dad wrote, "When I saw the car and thought of the loss and the hurt Princess Diana's kids and family would face, it brought back a flood of tears. I would like to tell you a few things about my princess, JoAnn, your mom."

I cried and laughed as I read his six-page single-spaced tribute to Mom.

Dad closed his e-mail by saying, "I didn't want to go on without her. Without God and the encouragement of your grandparents, I don't know how I would have made it. In many ways she still lives and we benefit. Yes, she has left us a heritage. She has shown us selfless love, adaptability, care for people, responsibility in difficult days without complaints, and a reaching out to do what she could. One day we will see her again face-to-face and be able to thank her for what she contributed and still contributes to our lives. Thank God for my princess."

That fall, as I thought of Princess Diana and Mom, God reminded me of the lasting legacy we, as women, can leave.

As we invest our lives in others, we leave a beautiful

legacy that continues to have impact on lives

for generations to come.

*L*ove the people I place in your path as you love yourself. Make the most of every opportunity, being wise in your treatment of strangers. May all of your conversations be full of grace, and seasoned with My love.

Patiently,

Your Heavenly Father

Matthew 22:39; Colossians 4:5–6

AN AFTERNOON WITH AMELIA

By Judy Carden

Settling into my seat on Flight 552 out of Detroit, the still little voice inside of me seemed to issue an alert that the afternoon would not go as I had hoped. In response to my "woman's intuition," my heart whispered but one request: *Please God . . . I need this time to work, no interruptions; just a little peace and quiet so that I can make my deadline.*

But God had other plans. I knew it the minute the flight attendant started down the aisle, a crying child in tow. Moments later she approached me. "Ma'am," she began in a hushed voice. "I'm sorry to disturb you, but I notice you are traveling alone and we have a 'situation' here. Amelia is also traveling alone, and, as you can see, is quite upset. Would it be alright if she sat next to you?"

I shelved all thoughts of making my deadline.

Slowly, my seven-year-old seatmate began to warm up to me. "My nickname is Amelia Bedelia," she volunteered. "I miss my daddy. I'm going to live with my mommy—they're divorced," she added softly.

13

"Bless your heart," I replied, realizing how cruel life could be when a little girl's heart is broken at about the same age she loses her first tooth.

A few minutes passed in silence before Amelia spoke again, "Wanna play beauty parlor? I have the stuff in my backpack." So, for the next two hours, this sweet child and I played "beauty parlor." First I French-braided her hair. Next, I painted Raspberry Rainbow polish on her nails, then, just before she fell asleep, I gently applied Galactic Grape gloss to her lips.

The last time I saw my little seatmate was in the baggage claim area. Spotting me, she tugged at her mother and pointed in my direction. I blew her an air kiss. She blew one back. Then my heart whispered another prayer—this time thanking God for interrupting my business world just long enough to be blessed by the sweet spirit of a little girl called "Amelia Bedelia."

How we should delight in the gift of

divine interruptions from the hustle

and bustle of the business world!

For they seem to whisper while we

work, saying to our hearts,

"Unwrap me—I am a sweet and

tender blessing just waiting

to be born."

*E*ven before you were conceived, I destined you for purpose! Your unveiled face reflects My glory. Even when you don't realize it, I'm transforming you into My likeness with an ever-increasing glory. I've given you a treasure in jars of clay to remind you that this all-surpassing power is from Me and not from you.

Gloriously,
Your Heavenly Father

———————————   ———————————

Psalm 139:16; 2 Corinthians 3:18; 2 Corinthians 4:7

ONLY MY UPS MAN
KNOWS FOR SURE

By Susan Duke

$\mathcal{I}$t was one of those bright, sunny, near-perfect days in May. My energy level was charged, and I was in the mood to do some serious housecleaning. *While I work,* I thought, *I'll try out my new green herbal facial mask, and condition my hair.*

Once I applied the green goop and placed my bright red shower cap over my conditioner-lathered hair, I was set. I cranked up the stereo with some lively soulful music, opened the doors and windows, grabbed a mop, pail, dust rag, and furniture polish, and started cleaning to the music.

I never heard the UPS truck pull into my back driveway—but as I twirled and danced through the kitchen, I stopped in my tracks at the sight of my brown-uniformed friend standing in the doorway. I ran to turn down the music and hurried back to the door.

"I'm sorry, I never heard you drive up," I said nonchalantly.

"I can see that, Ma'am," he offered, grinning broadly. "I have several items on the truck for you," he said, setting the first box on the porch.

Within minutes the faithful deliveryman had unloaded three huge toe sacks (burlap sacks) and five more boxes. On the outside of two of the boxes were cassette tape covers with my picture and name on them. Two other boxes, stamped with my name on the outside, contained books. And the last box was labeled . . . *Caution: Flammable Contents.*

"Quite a variety here today, Ma'am. I've never delivered toe sacks to anyone. I thought you might be a singer, because I've brought tapes to you before, but I have to admit, sometimes I wonder, Ma'am . . . just what all *do* you do?"

Suddenly, I caught a glimpse of my crackled green face in my sparkling glass door. "Well, I'm sure you'd never guess from today's appearance, but I'm a speaker, writer, and singer. And I make my own potpourri. The toe sacks contain wood shavings and the 'flammable' box contains essential oils."

"Are you a clown, too?" he chuckled, staring at my mud-dried face.

"No," I snickered, "just trying to get beautiful."

We are often labeled and defined by what we do. But God showed me something that day. We are not our labels. Speaking is not who I am. Neither is writing, or singing, or potpourri-making. These things are only a part of the sum total—green face and all, of the woman God created me to be.

We do not find our total identity in

what we do, but we are made complete

by using our multifaceted personali-

ties, gifts, and interests to fulfill our

God-given purpose.

*F*ocus on truth and noble things. Think about everything that is right, pure, and sweet. Reflect on whatever is admirable, excellent, or praiseworthy. Don't ever forget that you are My workmanship created in Jesus to do good works I've already prepared in advance for you to accomplish. When you believe in Me, I fill you with inexpressible joy.

Love,

Your God of Excellence

Philippians 4:8; Ephesians 2:10; 1 Peter 1:8

SOMETHING TO BELIEVE IN

By Judy Carden

Several years ago, Aubrey spent the afternoon snooping through old photo albums. "Hey, Mom!" she called. "Tell me the story about you and your friends in this picture."

Knowing exactly which picture she'd found, I dashed into the family room to look at the photograph, now faded with age.

"Okay, scoot over, Sweetie," I patted her arm. Settling beside Aubrey on the couch I shared with her once again the story about the greatest time of my life.

"I wasn't happy when, back in 1969, Mother told me she'd enrolled me at Our Lady of Mercy High School, an all-girls' academy in Rochester, New York. In fact, I had originally thought of sabotaging my entrance interview. But a funny thing happened while I sat in the principal's office.

"The sound of laughter echoed outside the office all during the meeting. I was surprised that girls could be happy living without guys at school. I sensed something special at Mercy and wanted to be part of it.

"Back then the nation was divided over the Vietnam War. Racial tensions thrived, and the *New York Times* said God was dead. I was fourteen and desperate for something to believe in. What impressed me most though was that no one at Mercy insisted I adopt their beliefs. They didn't have to. Their actions spoke volumes.

"They showed me that, contrary to media hype, God was very much alive, that a person's soul, rather than skin color, was what mattered, and that peace begins and ends within our own hearts. I learned the importance of loyalty, honor, and the courage to live one's convictions. I understood that by embracing those values I could change the world."

"Have you changed the world?" Aubrey interrupted.

Caressing the faded photograph in my hands I blinked back tears and said, "Because four hundred girls welcomed a knock-kneed fourteen-year-old with open arms, gave her something to believe in, and loved her, they encouraged me to make a difference in my corner of the world. As a wife and mother I change the world by molding and mending the hearts of those I love most. So, yes, Sweetie, I believe I have."

We all need something to do, someone

to love, and something to believe in.

Invest in the generation of tomorrow

today. Love a young person . . . all the

way to excellence!

$\mathcal{B}$e devoted to one another in brotherly love, honoring others above yourself. May all your words be wholesome, building others up according to their needs. Practice spiritual fervor as you serve Me. Show your hospitality to others using the special gifts I've given to you to faithfully administer My all-sufficient grace.

Graciously,

Your Heavenly Father

Romans 12:10–12; Ephesians 4:29; 1 Peter 4:9–10

A SOUTHERN LEGACY

By Susan Duke

"Look at these shirts," Jan said, while we shopped in a quaint gift store. Jan unfolded a soft blue-and-pink T-shirt with the embroidered initials G.R.I.T.S. "What does this mean?"

"Oh, that stands for Girls Raised in the South," I said.

"Well, I was raised in the North, so explain," Jan said.

For the next hour, over tea, I told Jan about black-eyed peas, grits, cornbread dressing, and being raised by a southern-to-the-bone mother.

"Mama always taught us girls a combination of southern charm and hard work. She said part of being a lady required learning to keep house so we'd know how when we were blessed with one of our own. My sisters and I had to hang out clothes, even when it was cold. But we also had sessions of practicing proper mannerisms—such as walking with a book on our heads so we'd learn to keep our chin up and walk with straight shoulders.

"We celebrated rare snow days in the South by making snow ice cream—and in the summer, we opened the windows and doors and picked elegant magnolia blossoms for Mama's mahogany dining table. I still remember my first drink from sweet, succulent honeysuckle flowers and the tang of fresh wild blackberries we picked in the woods."

Jan chimed in, "I've always admired the term 'southern charm.'"

"It's not that being raised in the South is any more special than being raised anywhere else," I said, "but Arthur Gordon, noted author, penned . . . 'Southerners had rather be charming than rich. They believe you can devote your energies to making money or being delightful, but you can't really do both.'"

We both laughed, as I said with all the southern charm I could muster, "And, darlin', those words make me feel soooo much better about not being rich!"

Mr. Gordon also states that southern charm is not an act, but rather a reaching out. "It's a small voice saying, 'Look, I'm aware of you. I know you're there. . . .'"

That's the main thing Mama instilled in me as a southern woman. With charming hospitality, she was at her best when prepared to serve and give her full attention to others. I guess you could say Mama taught me to *enjoy* being a woman . . . southern-style.

Our upbringings are part of who we are, and God has

equipped us with the ability to simply embrace and

celebrate our unique distinctions as women.

$\mathcal{M}$ay you rejoice in Me always. I've created each day for joy and gladness. I'll fill you with joy in My presence, with eternal pleasures at My right hand.

Joyously,
Your God of Abundant
Life

Philippians 4:4; Psalm 118:24; Psalm 16:11; John 10:10

"DEE DAH DAY"
MOMENTS

By LeAnn Weiss

"*H*ey, calories don't count on 'Dee Dah Day.' Let's order ice cream sundaes," Michelle said, as she and Teresa finished lunch.

"Sounds good to me," Teresa agreed.

Michelle and Teresa's spiritual discipline group was discussing John Ortberg's book, *The Life You've Always Wanted.* After reading the "Dee Dah Day" chapter about infusing childlike joy into life, their assignment was to devote a day to celebrating the simple things in life and then to journal what they did.

After tasty sundaes, the two women headed to St. Augustine, Florida, for their "Dee Dah Day" with cameras in hand to create a photo-essay for their assignment.

"Look! Let's climb the lighthouse," Teresa exclaimed, racing toward St. Augustine's landmark.

Reaching the top after mounting flights of stairs, the two friends enjoyed the cool ocean breeze from their bird's-eye view of Florida's oldest city. Teresa pointed to the remnants of an older abandoned lighthouse farther out in the water. Michelle said, "Isn't it great that God is our Lighthouse who never changes!"

Next, exploring St. Augustine, they wandered in and out of shops, mostly window-shopping. They bought souvenir rings to remember their day of celebration. Spotting a park with luscious green grass in the middle of the shopping center, Michelle and Teresa took off their shoes, letting the grass graze their toes as they took silly pictures of their feet.

The hot sun provided a perfect excuse to eat homemade ice cream in waffle cones. They walked barefoot along the beach, and didn't even mind being the only adults without kids to ride the carousel horses.

Nothing dampened their laughter-filled day, not even getting Teresa's car stuck in the sand during an early evening drive on the beach.

They headed home with a new understanding of what Ortberg meant when he penned, "Nothing is too small if it produces true joy in us and causes us to turn toward God in gratitude and delight." Today, Michelle and Teresa's "Dee Dah Day" photos remind them to be more carefree, and to notice God in the simple things of life.

Don't underestimate the importance of

balanced pleasure in spiritual

formation. Set aside time to

celebrate life's small joys.

*E*njoy life by honoring your earthly father. I'm able to turn the hearts of fathers to their daughters, and the hearts of daughters to their fathers.

Thinking Precious Thoughts of You, Your Abba Father

Ephesians 6:2–3; Malachi 4:6; Psalm 139:17

IN THE STILL OF THE NIGHT

By Judy Carden

$\mathcal{I}$t's difficult to dispute the face of truth. I've learned life's funny that way.

A few years back, in the still of the night, when the lights were low and all was quiet—in one of those moments that begs forgiveness and promises change, I thought of my father and how I had been neglecting our relationship.

Lord, I feel guilty about not seeing Dad more often. I'm busy though, juggling a family and a career—time is the one thing I can't give Dad right now. But even as the thoughts landed in my head, my conscience overruled them, whispering back, *Make time.*

The opportunity came sooner than I expected when our country club announced its upcoming father-daughter dinner dance.

Feeling more like a schoolgirl than a forty-year-old woman I phoned Dad and asked if he would escort me to the black-tie affair. "Why, I'd be honored," he replied, after a long moment.

I thought I heard him crying.

When our big night arrived I fretted, wondering if the strain that occurs between two people when the relationship is neglected would put a damper on the evening.

If Dad ever felt awkward, though, he was too much of a gentleman to let on. When the band began to play he grabbed me by the hand and said, "Come on, Princess! Let's show these folks how to dance!"

For the next three hours Dad twirled me around the dance floor, and I honestly couldn't recall the last time we'd had so much fun. We vowed we'd do it again someday soon.

Tonight it is late, the lights are low, the house is quiet, and, in another one of those moments—I think of Dad and feel sad that our *someday* hasn't happened sooner. I need no prompting. Though it's late, I call him and ask if he would escort me to the father-daughter dinner dance this February, still nine months away.

"I thought you'd never ask," Dad replies—but this time, the tears belong to me.

A father-daughter relationship is a

precious bond—but we must remem-

ber that it is a fragile love, and that,

left untended, it can wither and die.

The greatest gift a woman can give

her father is the gift of time.

Y ou've been justified by My all-sufficient grace. You can delight when you're feeling weak, insulted, persecuted, or when you're experiencing any kind of difficulty, remembering that My power is made perfect in your weakness. Because I help you, you won't be shamed or disgraced.

Love,
Your God of Amazing
Grace

Titus 3:7; 2 Corinthians 12:9–10; Isaiah 50:7

TRUE GRACE

By Susan Duke

$\mathcal{A}$lone in the doctor's combination bathroom/dressing room, I stepped out of the blue cotton gown and flushed the toilet, simultaneously reaching for my clothes and pantyhose hanging just above it on a hook.

I watched helplessly as my pantyhose slipped into the toilet bowl, swirled around, and headed south with a horrifying gurgle! *Oh, no! What am I going to do?*

I panicked!

After dressing as quickly as humanly possible, I snatched up my purse, shut the door, and headed for the receptionist's desk. As I smiled faintly and wrote a check for services rendered, I couldn't help thinking . . . *Poor doctor, this visit could cost him more than it cost me! I hope I haven't messed up the plumbing.* Looking back, I realize I should have come clean, confessed all, and accepted the consequences. But, the problem with imperfect moments is that they sneak up on us, take us by surprise, and before we know it, we've blown all semblance of dignity.

I've stood in crowds of influential people praying no one

would notice that I was wearing one navy and one black shoe. I've hugged strangers I mistook for friends. I've innocently checked out at Wal-Mart wearing a necklace I'd tried on with the tag in plain sight—realizing, once out the door, that I had gotten away with shoplifting! (Red faced, I walked back inside and handed over the merchandise. No arrest was made!)

I've come to the conclusion that the only way I can achieve real dignity in this life is by accepting that my quest for a perfect life is not immune to imperfect situations. While I'm amazed at the rush of embarrassing situations I can easily recall, I'm more amazed that God has innately equipped me to overcome . . . with true grace.

It's the kind of grace that unites the common and the elite—the meek and the mighty.

Jesus, though perfect, understands what imperfect situations and the sting of humiliation feel like. But because he was willing to walk, crawl, and stumble up a steep hill called Calvary—and give his life for our imperfection—*true grace* was born.

Awkward? I certainly think so. Did he overcome? Yes, indeed. Was it worth it?

You and I are living proof.

Realizing that real life is not perfect and that it has its

imperfect moments gives us the freedom to embrace

God's grace when we need it most.

I made you wonderfully. Internal beauty is what counts the most. Charm can be deceptive and outward beauty won't last forever, but when you respect Me, you are a woman deserving praise. Remember, any trials you experience are only temporary, and they have the power to refine your faith. Trials test your faith's genuineness, and they direct praise, glory, and honor to Me.

Making All Things
Beautiful in My Time,
Your God

Psalm 139:14; 1 Peter 3:3; Proverbs 31:30; 1 Peter 1:6–7

MORE THAN JUST
A PRETTY FACE

By Judy Carden

*A*s the bevy of beauties sashayed across the stage, grinning and winking at the judges, one pageant participant, my flaxen-haired daughter Aubrey (contestant number thirteen) was notably absent from the opening number.

I should have insisted that she back out of the pageant! I agonized. She had undergone extensive knee surgery just five days earlier.

But try as I might, Aubrey had refused to be deterred from her original plan. As a veteran of Miss Teen pageants, this was going to be her final curtain call—retiring from the pageant world before leaving for college.

As the other girls paraded about, I imagined Aubrey backstage with an ice bag on her bandaged knee. I feared I had erred by allowing her to participate.

When the time came for her to perform her talent, a brawny, handsome friend carried a frail but determined Aubrey onto the stage. With Brook carefully cradling her in his arms, she captivated the audience with a flawless performance of "When I Fall in Love."

The evening wear segment followed the talent portion. The girls, looking cool and confident, strutted around the stage, breathtaking gowns flowing behind their every step. Then came Aubrey. She hobbled out on her crutches, sweating profusely, dragging her bad leg the entire way. *Now I know I've made a mistake,* I grimaced, fighting back tears.

What happened next, I consider one of the single most defining moments of my daughter's rite of passage into womanhood. The master of ceremonies asked Aubrey if, under the circumstances, she had considered dropping the pageant. Adjusting the microphone, she said, "Yes, I did. But this final competition has been my dream. And even at my age, I understand that having a disability of any kind does not make me unworthy of beauty."

She placed as first runner-up. Of even greater significance, however, was that Aubrey dared to defy the odds—reminding the world that the worth of every young woman should be measured by much more than just physical attributes.

The true beauty of a woman is measured not because she "turns heads,"

but rather because she chooses to

touch hearts and inspire souls.

I'll equip you with everything good for doing My will. Praise Me with all of your heart, and tell others about all the wonderful things I've done. Don't be silent. Be glad, and let your heart sing praises to Me. Don't forget, you can do all things through Christ who strengthens you. Because I help you, you can sing in the refuge of My wings. When I call you, I'm faithful to follow through.

Love,

Your God Most High

————————— · —————————

Hebrews 13:20; Psalms 9:1–2; 30:12; 63:7;
Philippians 4:13; 1 Thessalonians 5:24

A SONG FROM MY HEART

By Susan Duke

$\mathcal{R}$esponding to an inner nudge, I put down my dish-towel and moved closer to the tape player on the kitchen table. As soft praise music played, I voiced a simple prayer—thanking God for walking my husband and me through a trying wilderness experience.

Just after moving to the country and building our log home, the real-estate economy collapsed and Harvey lost his contracting business. Circumstances became so bleak, we called ourselves Job and Jobetta! Through the trials, Harvey and I came to a place where we prayed, "Lord, if we lose everything, we'll still trust and serve you."

That afternoon in my kitchen, I felt God speaking to my heart, saying, "You will sing for me, Suzie."

"Lord, I'll always have a song of praise for you in my heart," I responded.

But God's urging resounded deeper within my soul. Now kneeling and sobbing, I remembered my promise to do whatever God called me to do. "But God, this is not on my multiple-choice list! Surely, you don't mean you want me to sing—literally! I've never sung—in school—in the choir . . . not even in the shower! How can I possibly do this? I'm not adequate."

"But I am," whispered God's gentle but not so small voice.

"Lord, if I'm really hearing from you, send me a teacher."

"I will be your Teacher," he urged.

The following Sunday, the music minister approached me saying, "Suzie, I want you to sing next Sunday." In the year we'd attended the church, he'd never mentioned music to me.

Sunday came. My knees were shaking, and my eyes closed as I sang my first song. Afterwards, I had the strange sense that God had been singing through me! I was only the vessel.

That first song from my heart was the birthing of Heartsong Ministries. One small beginning has now become a full-time speaking ministry to women across the United States. After thirteen years of speaking and singing at seminars, women's retreats, conferences, and churches of all denominations, I never forget that my heart's song was birthed not out of confidence in my own abilities, but of confidence in God's abilities.

God is able to do through us more

than we can dream or imagine, when

we surrender our wills and desires to

him. He is looking for available

vessels who will trust him to supply

whatever we need to heed his calling.

$\mathcal{I}$ 've designed you for relationships. Working together increases your productivity. When one of you stumbles or falls, the other is there for encouragement, inspiration, and support. May My favor rest upon you and establish the works of your hands.

Love,

Your God of Fellowship

Ecclesiastes 4:9–10; Psalm 90:17

MAKING WORK FUN

By LeAnn Weiss

$\mathcal{J}$ sat at my computer staring at the blank screen, feeling drained. *If I continue at this rate, I'll finish writing this book a year after my deadline,* I worried. Answering the phone, I recognized the cheery voice of my writing partner.

"Bob's going out of town on business," Judy said. "Why don't you drive down and spend the night, so we can work on our stories together?"

I could hear Judy's husband laughing in the background. "Dream on. You two will just stay up all night talking," Bob said, mocking our plans for a serious work session.

Later that day, I packed my suitcase and made the sixty-mile drive to Judy's house. Though we had spent time together at writer's conferences, and spoke nearly every day on the telephone, it was fun to finally see Judy's home and meet her family and friends.

First, we put the top down on Judy's sporty Chrysler convertible, donned sunglasses, cranked up the oldies music and sped off on a tour of quaint Winter Haven. Next, we exchanged story ideas while Judy baked several batches of her famous chocolate chip cookies.

Before we knew it, it was dinnertime. A seafood smorgasbord at her country club doubled as an opportunity to get to know Judy's sons better. After dinner we squeezed in an hour of work, but not wanting to disappoint Bob, we did stay up talking and laughing till the wee hours of the morning.

Judy didn't wake me up in the morning until she finished her three-mile jog. Then we decided we'd really better get to work. When one of us got stuck, we'd call out to the other, "What's the word I'm thinking of?" But that usually called for another round of laughter.

By the time Bob came home, we each had a few paragraphs to show from our brainstorming sessions.

But the real fruit and inspiration came when I arrived home refreshed—and almost effortlessly zipped out three new stories.

As women, God has made us uniquely

relational. Just talking and being

together is nourishment for our souls.

$\mathscr{A}$ccept wherever I've placed you. Being happy in your work is a gift from Me. I'll keep you occupied with gladness of heart. Let joy, love, peace, patience, kindness, goodness, faithfulness, gentleness, and self-control radiate from your life. The unfading beauty of a gentle and quiet spirit is of great worth in My eyes. You'll find amazing results when you employ patience and gentleness.

Love,

Your God of All Joy and

Peace

———————— ❋ ————————

Ecclesiastes 5:19–20; Galatians 5:22–23; 1 Peter 3:4; Proverbs 25:15

SERVING UP JOY

By Judy Carden

$\mathcal{I}$ took the job out of desperation. Fresh out of college, my heart's desire had been fashion modeling, but the offers weren't exactly pouring in. That's when a friend told me about a waitress position that was available at a trendy restaurant in nearby Hollywood, Florida. There was just one glitch: I wasn't sure I was cut out to serve others. However, fearing eviction more than failure, I accepted the position.

My first few weeks were disastrous. I tripped and fell—tray in hand—on numerous occasions. Large orders flustered me. Customers complained about everything. I was utterly miserable—as the lone waitress on a staff with experienced waiters.

One evening, during the dinner rush, born out of my immediate need for survival, I began flooding heaven with urgent petitions for patience and a gentle spirit. It wasn't long before a metamorphosis took place, and I began to relax.

Over the next ten months, I eventually mastered handling those large orders. I learned the art of food presentation and served dishes promptly. I bussed tables and mopped up various spills of unknown origin. The biggest change, though, came in the way I treated the customers; so much so that many of the regular patrons requested that they only be seated in my station. I had finally won them over. A gentle, joyous spirit had taken seed in my soul.

But it wasn't until my last day on the job when one of the regulars, an elderly gentleman, presented me with a corsage and a note that I realized the impact I had made. The note read: "You are the warmest young woman I have ever had the pleasure of knowing and the reason many of us frequent this establishment. I have enjoyed observing you celebrate life."

Years later, each time I feel trapped in a struggle with my "sense of self," a carnation corsage and a customer's affirming words come to mind. And before too long, the kinder, gentler version of me, the woman God desires me to be, returns to celebrate life.

A gentle, joyous spirit is often the tender trademark of a

godly woman—for when we allow God to pour his

gentle joy deep within our hearts, others will

sense God's love through us.

$\mathcal{W}$hen you secure your confidence in Me, you are blessed. Remember, your strength is not by might or power, but by My Spirit. I'll strengthen your heart so that you'll be blameless and holy in My presence. My joy will be your strength.

Fortifying You,
Your God and Fortress

Jeremiah 17:7; Zechariah 4:6; Isaiah 41:10;
Nehemiah 8:10

STEEL MAGNOLIAS

By Susan Duke

$\mathcal{G}$athered around Joanna's table in her quaint butter-cup-yellow dining room, my friends and I had just finished one of Joanna's famous home-cooked dinners. "You did it again, Joanna," we agreed. "Your corn chowder is the best."

When Joanna, Brenda, Janice, and I get together, we always have plenty to talk about, plenty to eat, and plenty of blessings to count. While we all keep busy schedules, the four of us set aside special days during the year to meet at one of our homes. We may cook up our favorite foods, watch funny videos, or just "hang out" and catch up on each other's lives. Occasionally, when Joanna creates a fabulous dinner, our husbands join us. Today was one such time.

Smiling and looking across the table rather pensively, Joanna's husband, Robert, said, "I've never told you this, but I've named you four the '*Steel Magnolias.*'"

"'*Steel Magnolias*'? Like in the movie? Why, Robert?" we all asked.

"You all live in different towns and don't get together that often, but when you do, there's an atmosphere of strength and strong sense of loyalty that prevails. Your friendship is strong as steel."

Robert was also referring to critical occasions when we've gathered to pray and support one of our group during a crisis, riding out the storm together—like the friends in *Steel Magnolias*—counting on each other's laughter, tears, compassion, and hands-on help to carry us through.

"I once read that 'women are like tea bags…you never know how strong they are until they get into hot water!'" I said.

We all laughed, but told Robert we appreciated his choice of words—*women of strength*, rather than *strong women*—and then we discussed the difference. The term *strong women* could mean cold, hard, tough, or controlling. The term *women of strength* implies drawing confidence, inner strength, and the gift of encouragement and nurturing from God.

"Let me assure you," Robert concluded, "you are the latter—*women of strength*—gentle as magnolia blossoms, but with the strength of steel."

I looked at my friends' radiant faces and then spoke for all of us. "Thanks, Robert. We'll accept that as a compliment—not only to us, but to God, for giving us the gift and courage to be both."

God gives women the natural ability

to nurture, support, and exhibit

compassion while standing in the

strength of his uncompromising

power and grace.

$\mathcal{B}$e strong and let your heart take courage as you hope in Me. A true friend brings earnest counsel. As iron sharpens iron, so is the influence of a godly woman.

Filling Your Heart,
God

———————————   ———————————

Psalm 31:24; Proverbs 20:5; 27:9, 17

WOMAN TO WOMAN

By Judy Carden

$\mathcal{I}$ had been wrestling with unresolved grief after the death of my husband, when my pastor offered to put me in touch with a colleague of his. "She's a great woman; you'll like her," he assured me. I smiled politely when he handed me a sheet of paper with the woman's name and long-distance telephone number on it. Dropping it into my purse, I wondered, *How can this woman, whom I've never even met, possibly help me?* But I thanked my pastor just the same.

I was surprised when, several days later Celia phoned *me*. Vibrant and warm, just as my pastor had promised, Celia immediately put my mind at ease. "I've worked through the grieving process several times," she shared, "I understand your pain."

I shared with her how I was emotionally depleted—too busy tending to everyone else's wounds to deal with my own.

After our conversation Celia wrote a letter to me. "We women tend to nurture others first; often ignoring our own pain," she wrote. "A common mistake is to leap from a head understanding of a deep pain to saying to ourselves: 'everything is fine now that I understand.' Then, we wonder why our bodies shut down and dreams begin to repeat themselves. When we run out of strength to keep pushing 'stuff' down within, darkness occurs. And in the darkness comes our temptation to grab for the quick fix; to mistake the fireflies for the dawn."

The letter offered me tremendous insight as to why I was emotionally and spiritually depleted, and helped me find the courage to work through a long and painful process. And though Celia didn't know me personally, she understood what mattered most—the state of my heart.

Nearly eleven years have passed since I received Celia's letter. Although we never met, her remarkable gifts of wisdom and compassion helped me a great deal. Woman to woman, life is a gentler journey when one of us holds the torch in order that the other, stumbling in the darkness, might find her way into the light.

A heart-to-heart connection, not a

face-to-face encounter, defines the

common bond intertwining the

language of our souls.

*B*ecause you are in Me, you experience newness. May you grow in faith, goodness, knowledge, self-control, perseverance, godliness, brotherly kindness, and love. When you increase in these qualities, you won't be ineffective and unproductive in your knowledge of Me, and you'll never fall. Perceive the new things I'm doing!

Inspiring You,
Your God of Light

2 Corinthians 5:17; 2 Peter 1:5–11; Isaiah 43:19

CYBER-TALK

By Susan Duke

"*D*o you have e-mail?" a new friend asked recently.

"Are you kidding?" I responded. "*Neither rain nor snow, nor dark of night shall keep me from my appointed rounds . . .* of delivering or retrieving my e-mail!" (My version of the postman's creed.)

Women's inherent need for communicating gives us all the motivation we need for jumping into the world of Macs, modems, and mice. These days I'm answering more e-mails than phone calls. But if the computer weren't necessary to my writing career, I'm afraid I'd still be asking my cyber-savvy friend, Kathy, "*What is e-mail, anyway?*" She laughingly reminds me of my early writing days when I rebelled at flipping the "on" switch of my first computer.

"I haven't typed since high school," I whined to Kathy. "I'll always be a longhand writer . . . and can't imagine trying to type what I'm thinking—someone will just have to type for me."

Now, nine books later, I can't imagine life—or writing—

without a computer. E-mail is imperative to communicating with editors, writing partners, family, and friends. My husband shakes his head in disbelief as he watches my fingers fly effortlessly across the keyboard—remembering the frustrating hunt-and-peck days of my cyber-rebellion.

Even my eighty-year-old mom has taken the cyberspace plunge, succumbing to her womanly instinct of refusing to be held back by newfangled ways of communicating. While setting up her computer, she asked excitedly, "Does this mean I'll have my own *dot com*?" Her eighty-six-year-old newlywed husband, Bill, who doesn't hear well, mistook what Mama said and asked, "Did you say *it's gonna be a dark night*?"

It's thrilling to see Mama step into new horizons of communicating, and I still laugh when I click "get mail" and find a message from Mama saying, "Hello! It's a dark night here . . . how about there?"

I'll never fully understand cyber-lingo, and it's still confusing when my husband fluently talks about hard drives, scanning for viruses, downloading programs, and upgrading memory. (Oh, if he could only do that for my brain!) But as long as I'm supplied with cyber-power—and God's power keeps me supplied with inspiration—I'll keep writing, embracing new challenges, and relishing the joyous bliss of cyber-talk.

Isn't it nice to know God has equipped

us with enough flexibility to learn

new methods of expression? When we

step beyond the limitations of old

ways of thinking, God can lead us to

new horizons of exciting possibilities.

$\mathcal{I}$'ll instruct you and teach you the best way for you. I intimately know you. I'll counsel you and watch over you. My Spirit will guide you into all truth. Test everything and hold on to the good. Hear My voice and follow Me.

Guiding You,
Your Good Shepherd

———————— • ————————

Psalm 32:8; Psalm 18:32; John 16:13;
1 Thessalonians 5:21; John 10:27

CHOOSING GOD'S BEST

By LeAnn Weiss

Life was busy but good. After months of odds-and-ends jobs, I received a number of exciting career and ministry opportunities. Not wanting to disappoint anyone, I tried to figure out a way to accept them all. But eventually, I came to the conclusion that no matter how I juggled my schedule, there weren't enough hours in the day to squeeze them all in.

I wonder what Mom and Dad would advise? I thought, as I realized I was going to have to make some decisions. Because my parents are missionaries and live in East Africa, picking up the phone wasn't economical, costing nearly two dollars a minute. Mail service to Africa was extremely slow and unreliable. Unfortunately, e-mail wasn't developed for widespread use yet, so contact with my parents was usually restricted to birthdays and major holidays.

Later that day, I received an envelope from Africa. My mom had enclosed some prayer bulletins for me to read. On top was a yellow Post-It note with this handwritten message: "My dear LeAnn—You are a precious daughter. Be blessed with discernment, with the ability to choose God's best over the good, with joy! Much Love, Mom."

Mom's message gave me fresh insight into what I had been reading earlier that morning in my quiet time. I read that Jesus said to his Father, "I have brought you glory on earth by completing the work you gave me to do" (John 17:4).

Jesus could have been frenzied by the endless opportunities he faced to heal people and to meet needs, but instead he focused on God's agenda for his life, free from others' expectations.

As I reread Mom's message, I picked up the phone and politely declined some opportunities, sensing that while they were good, they weren't God's best for me.

Examining the postmark on the envelope, I saw that Mom had mailed her short message almost six months earlier. I prayed: "*God, you knew this was exactly the message I needed today. Thanks for Mom's sensitivity to your prompting months ago. May your best always be the filter of my priorities.*"

As women, we're known for our uncanny intuition.

When we use our God-given sensitivity to hear and

respond to his still small voice, God can mightily use us

as ambassadors of his divine direction.

*C*ome to me when you're tired and overwhelmed. I'll give you rest. Follow My ways, and I'll show you how to live freely with less stress. I refresh the weary and satisfy the faint. Repent and turn to Me so that you may experience times of refreshing from Me.

Restoring You,
God

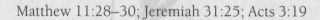

Matthew 11:28–30; Jeremiah 31:25; Acts 3:19

MAKING OUR OWN MAGIC

By Judy Carden

$\mathcal{F}$or weeks I had been on systems overload—both mind and body beaten down from the demands I had placed on myself as a working wife and mother. Just when I thought I couldn't make one more deadline, prepare one more meal, wash one more load of laundry, or soothe one more restless heart, I came down with a cold.

Lord, I can't continue at this pace. Show me some way to take a break . . . whimpered my weary soul as I warmed some chicken noodle soup in the microwave. Then, forcing myself to sip the steaming soup, the thought of a bubble bath came to my mind.

I visualized the *perfect* bubble bath in an oversized, sunken bathtub. Color-coordinated bubbles and bath beads in a glass jar. An array of lighted aromatherapy candles artistically arranged around the room. Classical music piped in through the sound system. A cup of hot tea with honey awaiting me. It was a setting fit for a queen, and it was just calling my name.

Encouraged, I rummaged through a messy kitchen drawer, grabbing the only candle I could find. Filling a plastic tumbler with diet ginger ale and throwing a few animal crackers on a Batman plate, I headed toward my undersized bathroom with the cracked tub. I borrowed the boys' radio, set it to an "easy listening" station, and filled the tub with hot water and bubbles.

After soaking in a sea of bubbles for awhile, something remarkable happened: The tiny bathroom seemed to grow. The crack in the tub vanished. The radio sounded more like the symphony. And when I closed my eyes, I was not only *in* my imaginary setting fit for a queen—I *was* the queen!

Stepping from the tub, refreshed and rejuvenated, I smiled, realizing that sometimes we have to be willing to meet God halfway when we are seeking simplicity from our stressful world. He provides the moment, and then we must make a little magic of our own!

Sometimes a simple indulgence—a

long bath, a cup of cinnamon tea, or

curling up on a lounge chair with a

good book—is all we need to escape

from the "hurry" of our world,

allowing us to rest our souls and

open our hearts to God.

$\mathcal{I}$ know the plans I have for you. My plans are to help you prosper, not to harm you. I'll restore your soul and lead you in paths of righteousness. When you seek Me with all your heart, you'll find Me. I'll bring you to a hope-filled future, leading you home with cords of human kindness and ties of love.

Love,

Your God of All Hope

Jeremiah 29:11–14; Psalm 23:3; Hosea 11:4

GOING HOME

By Susan Duke

The last morning in her Texas home, Pat awakened with mixed feelings of eager expectancy and sadness. She and her husband, having made a life-changing decision to move back to Pat's hometown in Tennessee, would be leaving by mid afternoon.

When Pat called to say good-bye, I asked, "Is there time to meet for a quick breakfast visit before you leave?"

"That's exactly what I need," Pat said. "We're actually ahead of schedule, and I can't think of anything I'd rather do while Neal ties up loose ends."

While enjoying hot coffee and a delicious country breakfast, Pat shared her deepest thoughts about going back "home" to Tennessee. Hearing about the painful events in her past, I could fully understand why the move had been such a challenging decision. Pat and two brothers had endured the death of their mother and a tumultuous childhood at the hands of their father before he died. Going home for Pat meant reuniting with her brothers, but it also meant dredging up unpleasant memories in her heart that might not yet be fully healed.

"Suzie, I'm trying to trust that being drawn back to the very place I wanted to run away from when I was younger is God's leading."

As we talked, I sensed God's presence. "Pat, even though I'll miss you terribly, I think God has many wonderful plans for your life. Because you're willing to open your heart and go back home, God is going to restore your joy and your relationships, and heal your memories."

"I feel that, Suzie. That's why I have to go."

As we said our good-byes, God prompted me to slip a delicate silver heart locket from around my neck. "Here," I said tearfully, as I placed the necklace around Pat's neck, "this is a reminder that God is leading your heart home to fill it with healing and hope."

Today, Pat is enjoying the restoration of family relationships and her newly built home, and has founded a wonderful outreach ministry in her community. I love receiving Pat's letters and e-mails that testify to God's faithfulness. She often mentions the necklace, saying it is a constant reminder that God has indeed helped her heart find its way home.

God is not only the God of the future,

but the God of our past. When we

allow God access to our hearts and

trust him for complete healing

and restoration, our hearts

are truly "home."

I've engraved you on the palms of My hands, loving you with an everlasting love that reaches to the heavens. You are able to love because I first loved you. May love always be your motivation. When you love one another, I live in you and My perfect love is made complete in you.

Blessings,
Your God of Love

———————— ⚬ ————————

Isaiah 49:16; Psalm 36:5; 1 John 4:12, 19;
1 Corinthians 16:14

AS LOVE UNFURLS

By Judy Carden

$\mathcal{I}$t's 9:00 A.M., and Aubrey has phoned me four times. Normally, my college sophomore, who lives four hours from home, phones once or twice a day, but she has just jumped, heart first, into a strange new world of love, and her spirit is spilling over with joy.

"Oh, Mom," she gushed during an earlier conversation. "He is the most *incredible* guy I have ever met! He's just like me, except that he's a guy, of course—he *really* loves God, sports, and country music. He's handsome, smart, fun, *and* he's hopelessly old-fashioned, just like me!"

Stopping only to catch her breath, she continued, "I can't concentrate. I feel like I'm floating on a cloud and I replay everything he says to me over and over again in my mind. Oh, Mommy, I have to go to class now, but can you tell I'm smiling?"

Can I tell she is smiling? Not only can I tell she is smiling, I can feel her heart racing. I can envision the extra spring in her step and hear the sweet song in her soul.

The mother in me wants to caution her to hang on to her heart—for she is young, and naïve. But she's not looking for a lecture; she's inviting me into her world!

So, instead, I listen. I share with her that when a woman falls in love, life is one delightful rush after another. It's violins and wildflowers. Moonlit nights and fireworks. It's whispering his name and wondering why you never realized before what a beautiful name it is. It's holding hands and exchanging glances. And dreaming of a future together.

I marvel as love reveals itself to her. As each moment of their tenderness unfurls I am reminded there is no mystery…no miracle…no wonder… greater than love. And I thank God my daughter chose me as a trusted confidante to accompany her on the maiden voyage of her heart.

The power of love is unmistakable, for

when love enters our heart it trans-

forms us—leaving an indelible

imprint of tenderness on our soul.

$\mathcal{D}$on't compare yourself to others. You're only required to measure up to the plans I have for you. I've given you unique gifts, according to My grace. I cause all things, even the things that initially seem bad, to work together for your good when you love Me and are called according to My purpose. You'll rest in the shadow of the Almighty when you dwell in My shelter.

Love,

Your God Most High

——————— ⬤ ———————

2 Corinthians 10:12–13; Romans 12:6; Romans 8:28;
Psalm 91:1

KEEPING THE HOME
FIRES BURNING

By Susan Duke

"*H*oney, can you come home," I sobbed on the phone to my husband. "Now?"

"What's wrong?" Harvey asked with deep concern.

"I kind of caught the kitchen on fire!" I wailed.

When he arrived on the scene, he was relieved to find less damage than my trembling voice had portrayed. After working a few hours in my home office, I'd gone into the kitchen to cook some bacon for a sandwich. The portable phone (which normally rests on a base in the kitchen) rang in the living room.

In the seconds it took to answer the phone, I smelled smoke. I ran back into the kitchen just as my stove, vent-a-hood, and wooden cabinets burst into flames. By the time I reached the stove, the fire had extinguished itself.

It turned out to be one of those all-things-work-together-for-good situations. Our insurance man determined that the smoke damage warranted replacing the cabinets, our fifteen-year-old stove, and outdated dishwasher. I wouldn't exactly recommend this sort of home remodeling, but I accepted it as a merciful blessing.

Whenever we travel down memory lane, Harvey reminds me of another kitchen disaster we survived one Saturday afternoon when I whipped up our family's favorite dessert—pineapple upside-down cake. When the timer rang, I carefully removed the long, glass, baking pan from the oven and set it on the stovetop to cool. It smelled scrumptious. Waiting in the family room, we counted the moments before our cake was cool enough to serve.

That's when we heard the explosion.

"What's that?" Harvey asked, rushing to the kitchen. "Oh no! Oh no!" he groaned.

The cake had blown up! Unknowingly, I'd set the dish on a burner that was turned on low. The Pyrex dish shattered—embedding cake and glass in a gazillion pieces all over the walls, ceiling, floor, and countertops.

Thankfully, Harvey is great at cleaning *and* cooking. I recently bought him a little sign that hangs by our new stove: "Real Men Wear Aprons, Buddy." He loves it—and says I've proven that a woman's place is not necessarily in the kitchen—but there are plenty of other ways to keep the home fires burning.

As women, our homemaking ambition doesn't

necessarily mean striving to fit into traditional domestic

roles, but celebrating the uniqueness of God's custom

role for us individually.

*R*emember life is more important than food and your body is more important than clothes. Don't worry about anything. I faithfully take care of the smallest details, even clothing the lilies with splendor and feeding the little sparrows. I know all of your needs, and you can trust Me to provide according to My riches in glory. When you delight yourself in Me, I bless you with the very desires of your heart.

Love,

Your 100 Percent

Faithful God

Matthew 6:25–30; Philippians 4:19; Psalm 37:4

A PERFECT FIT

By LeAnn Weiss

$\mathcal{W}$hen Gail first heard that a date had been set for her church's Second Annual Volunteer Appreciation Banquet, she immediately recalled the excitement of the previous year's banquet. The churchwomen had gone all out, donning spectacular semi-formal to formal evening gowns for the banquet.

I have six months to save. Maybe I can afford to buy a special dress for the banquet.

Months later Gail opened her official golden-embossed invitation to the banquet. She looked in her checkbook and sighed. Raising seven children, Gail just couldn't save much. *I guess I'll just have to be content wearing the same dress I wore last year.*

Meanwhile, when Ginny received her invitation, she rummaged through her closet. She discovered a dress that she had bought for last year's banquet and never worn. It still had the price tag attached. Ginny tried it on, but it didn't look right. She decided to shop for a new dress.

I'll give the other dress away, Ginny thought.

As she prayed about who might need a new dress at church, Gail kept coming to her mind. So Ginny called Gail and arranged to give her the dress at church the next Sunday.

Ginny smiled when she saw Gail wearing the stunning navy blue shift dress with a beaded chiffon overlay at the banquet. "Gail, it's a perfect fit," Ginny complimented. "It looks so much better on you than me."

"Thanks. I just made a few alterations to the sleeves, and I already had shoes that were a perfect match," Gail replied.

As the banquet started, Gail silently paused to acknowledge the real giver, "God, I know I'm wearing a love gift from you. Thanks for giving me the desire of my heart in such a beautiful way."

God doesn't just care about our

basic needs. He loves surprising us

with even our smallest heart desires

when we yield the details to him.

*W*hen you forgive a wrong, you promote unconditional love. Bear with each other and forgive the things that hurt you, just like I forgive you. I demonstrated My unlimited love for you by loving you while you were still a sinner. I remove your sin from you as far as the east is from the west, filling you with love able to cancel a multitude of shortcomings.

Mercifully,

Your Savior

Proverbs 17:9; Colossians 3:13; Romans 5:8;
Psalm 103:12; 1 Peter 4:8

THE PEN OF FORGIVENESS

By Judy Carden

$\mathcal{I}$t was the night before Christmas, and a soft blanket of snow had just begun to cover the earth when Caroline accidentally uncovered a secret that would forever change her life: Her beloved husband of twenty-six years had been unfaithful to their marriage.

Stunned, Caroline curled up on a corner of their bedroom floor. In the living room, her husband and six children merely walked through the motions of Christmas, aware that something was terribly wrong. Suddenly, Caroline felt a soft, still voice whisper to her broken heart: *You hold the pen of life in your hand—it is you who must write the words to this script—you who will create an ending to this story.*

She wrapped an afghan around herself as another wave of grief washed over her, and she fought to remember exactly when she and the man she still loved became two strangers living under one roof. *Is this what is to become of us now? Nothing more than a midlife marriage shattered by the unthinkable?* But hadn't she sensed a hollow silence between them? That they had grown indifferent to each other? Or even that her husband had tried, in vain, to re-create the magic that once existed between them?

93

Caroline thought of her children, and that, if she chose to, she could give her family the gift of a future together. *So, it all comes down to this,* she reasoned. *I've got the pen and I'm the one who writes the script.*

In what was the most powerful moment of their marriage, she made the choice to forgive her husband. Realizing the journey ahead would be filled with challenges, she opted still to embrace the future rather than the past. For though the pain from his unfaithfulness was almost more than she could bear, Caroline knew that without forgiveness, bitterness is all they would have to show for a lifetime of love.

So on the tattered page of her husband's heart, in the story of their life, she inscribed the words, *I forgive you* and trusted that God, the Father of forgiveness, would guide her to write the rest.

Forgiveness is releasing the other

person's failure from the sanctuary of

our soul, freeing us to compose mag-

nificent manuscripts in the stories

of our lives.

Love each other deeply from the heart. I help put lonely people into families, uniting hearts to suffer and celebrate together. Don't forget, I'm with you always, to the very end of the age.

Uniting Hearts,

God

_____   _____

1 Peter 1:22; Psalm 68:6; 1 Corinthians 12:26–27;
Matthew 28:20

HEART TIES

By Susan Duke

$\mathcal{I}$n 1986, Sharon signed up for swimming classes at the local YWCA. On the first night she met Maria. Sharon was drawn to Maria's personality and her Polish accent. After the class, Sharon asked, "Would you like to go have some tea?"

"I'd love to," Maria replied.

Sharon and Maria connected immediately. As they exchanged stories about their lives, they found the similarities to be uncanny. They were the same age. Sharon's mother's family and Maria were from the same tiny town in Poland. Maria's father, his family, and Sharon's mother's family all shared the same last name. They even had the same coloring, height, and weight!

Months passed and their friendship grew. It was strange how they would sometimes meet and be wearing an identical piece of clothing or matching shoes. Since Maria's only living relative, her mother, was in Warsaw, Poland, Maria felt as if she'd found a sister and soul mate in Sharon.

When Maria adopted a daughter—two-year-old Alexa Ray—from Poland, Sharon became a part of Ali's life from the moment she came to America. Although Sharon hadn't heard or spoken Polish since childhood, she understood everything little Ali said.

It was as if Ali had been blessed with two moms. Sharon and her husband were named godparents and shared all the "firsts," privileges normally reserved for parents only. But Maria willingly shared her heart and her daughter with Sharon.

Maria nursed Sharon through a painful divorce, calling her daily to offer love and support. A year later, Sharon returned the nurturing compassion when Maria's own marriage fell apart.

When Sharon healed and got remarried to a wonderful man, Ali asked Sharon, "Will he be my new godfather?"

"Of course!" said Sharon.

Ali, now fourteen, often comes to Sharon for advice and "venting" sessions typical of teenagers.

More than a friendship, Sharon and Maria share a sister-hood, a heart-to-heart, God-thing bond like no other relationship either has ever known. Maria and Sharon know, by God's own hand, they are family—connected at heart.

We are all a part of God's family and a

much larger circle than our immediate

family. God sometimes arranges

divine encounters to give us "heart

ties" that enrich and bless our lives.

*E*xperience the healing power
of laughter. Enjoy the continual
feast of a cheery heart.

Joyfully,

Your God

—————— ⬩ ——————

Proverbs 17:22; Proverbs 15:15

Girls Just Want to Have Fun

By Judy Carden

Nurturing someone back to health after gallbladder surgery is serious business that requires making the patient rest. At least that's what Bob thought eight years ago when he left me in my friend Lenore's care while he worked at a weekend retreat for men.

"I'm afraid things won't be as calm as at home," Bob admitted the evening before the retreat, after Lenore had volunteered to oversee my convalescence. "It's not too late for me to cancel—"

"Nonsense!" I cut him off. "They're counting on you, and besides, I can rest at Lenore's house just as easily as I can rest at ours."

The next morning, after dropping the children at school and me at Lenore's, a skeptical Bob left town.

Lenore insisted that I immediately climb into bed while she unpacked my suitcases and got the children's things situated. Shortly after, she returned with a glass of ginger ale and a stack of magazines.

"Can I get you anything else, Sugar?" Lenore asked as she turned to leave.

"Yes. You can get me to the mall. But first call Joy and Kathy and see if they can meet us in town for lunch. I'll go stark-raving mad if I have to lie still one more day."

Lenore stopped in her tracks. "No way!" she protested. "Bob will be furious."

"We won't tell him," I coaxed. "Until afterwards, that is. Pleeease!"

"Well, alright," Lenore conceded. "But remember, this was *your* idea."

On our way to the mall I spotted a bumper sticker that said: "My husband says he'll leave me if I don't stop shopping. Boy, I'll miss that man."

That was the final piece of inspiration I needed. My girls-just-*need*-to-have-fun personality emerged, and remained until Bob returned a few days later and I resumed my role as the placid patient.

Bob never knew until much later that Lenore and I took a U-turn approach to his rest-only philosophy. And while what he didn't know at the time didn't hurt *him* . . . my four days of fun with gal pals revived my droopy spirits and certainly helped me!

Sometimes, a healthy dose of fun with friends is good for

what ails us. Laughter really is a most effective medicine

for the soul!

$\mathcal{I}$ redeem your life from the pits of life, crowning you with love and compassion. My compassion for you is fresh every morning. May you be kind and compassionate to others. Remember, whatever you do for the least of these brothers and sisters, it's just like you're serving Me. When you give yourself to meet the needs of the hungry and oppressed, you shine in My eyes.

Love,

Your God of

Compassion

Psalm 103:4; Lamentations 3:22–23; Ephesians 4:31; Matthew 25:40; Isaiah 58:10

MISS SARAH'S PIANO

By Susan Duke

Sarah hadn't paid much attention to the shabbily dressed man standing inside the downtown café's foyer until he ambled over to a piano that sat against the wall. While waiting to be served, she observed his fingers brush the keys. He sat down and started playing a beautiful melody. Moments later, the café's owner walked over, grabbed the man's elbow, and angrily ushered him out the front door.

Sarah tried ignoring the thud that hit her spirit while watching the scene. Owning an exquisite Italian restaurant herself, she understood about catering to certain clientele—and reasoned that the café owner had every right to ask the bedraggled man to leave.

Two weeks later, Sarah saw the raggedy man on a sidewalk bench. "What's your name?" she asked.

"Bert."

Sarah retrieved a business card from her purse. "Bert, I have a restaurant a few blocks from here and a piano that no one ever plays. If you're ever in the area, you're welcome to come in and play for me."

Bert's gnarled, shaky hand reached for the card. "Thanks," he said.

To Sarah's surprise, three days later, a clean-shaven Bert walked into her restaurant. "I'm here to play your piano, Ma'am," Bert said, "before the crowd comes of course."

Sarah smiled and led Bert to the piano. Bert played for an hour . . . one beautiful, heart-lilting melody after another. Sarah brought him a plate and asked, "Bert, will you play through dinner?"

"You sure, Ma'am?" Bert questioned.

"Bert, I don't know what happened to you, but someone with your talent shouldn't be living on the streets," Sarah said.

"Miss Sarah, my life took a bad turn some years back and the music left . . . until that day in the café. Then you invited me here and I heard it again . . . way down in my soul."

That night, as Bert played, customers applauded, slipped him song requests, and piled money on top of the piano to show their appreciation of the fine musician.

Through one woman's compassion, God restored Bert's life-long passion and gave him hope. Today, Bert is no longer homeless and plays for restaurants and special events throughout the city.

The power of compassion is

amazing. When God stirs our soul,

a simple act of kindness can

change a life and bring healing

and hope to a heart.

I bless you on every occasion, fueling you to reach out to others. Encourage and build each other up daily. Spur others on to love and good deeds. Remember, with the measure that you invest your life in the lives of others, I'll give back to you. As you refresh others, I'll refresh you.

Generously,

Your God of Eternal Encouragement

———————   ———————

2 Corinthians 9:11; Hebrews 3:13; 10:24;
1 Thessalonians 5:11; Luke 6:38; Proverbs 11:25

WRITE FROM THE HEART

By LeAnn Weiss

$\mathcal{M}$idsummer as I sorted through a mountain of mail that had accumulated during my month-long trip to Africa, Susan Duke's Heartsong Ministries business card caught my eye. Susan had been so warm, genuine, charming, and friendly when we had talked and exchanged business cards the last day of the Florida Writers Conference.

She must have an interesting story I could interview her about, I thought as I dialed her Texas number. I was in the middle of writing my first book, *Hugs for Friends*, and needed another story.

Talking to Susan was like talking to a lifelong friend and kindred spirit. During our laughter-filled interview, we discussed the projects we were working on. When she discovered I wasn't part of a writing group, Susan said, "Hey, if you'd like, you can e-mail me your stories and I'll show you how to self-edit."

Struggling as a fledgling writer and knowing she had received the award for Best Work Submitted at the conference where we met, I couldn't refuse the offer. Susan took me under her wing and taught me, line by line, how to improve my writing. Our telephone mentoring partnership quickly developed into a friendship that has been a lifeline from God. She's the rare type of friend who exemplifies every attribute of friendship.

We've exchanged hundreds of e-mails. When I'm burning the midnight oil and my computer announces, "You've got mail," I know it's 'Suzie' on-line with an encouraging note. We spend hours each week on the phone sharing, laughing, praying, brainstorming, and encouraging each other. Her incredible heart for God keeps me accountable. I've even stayed at Suzie and her husband Harvey's home in Texas.

I was so excited when my publisher followed my suggestion and enlisted Susan to coauthor the *Heartlifters* series with me. Working together again on this *God Things Come in Small Packages* series, there's no doubt in my mind that exchanging business cards with Susan was one of the biggest "God things" in my life. I couldn't have dreamed of a better collaborator. Next to Jesus, her friendship has been my major inspiration, "the wind beneath my wings." We didn't just exchange business cards; we exchanged hearts.

God gives women unique opportuni-

ties to mentor others, making heart

connections that will change lives.

$\mathcal{M}$y precious daughter, make time to be still and know that I am God. I have redeemed you and called you by name. Wisdom that comes from Me is pure, peace loving, considerate, submissive, full of mercy and good fruit, impartial, and sincere. When you wait and hope upon Me, I'll renew your strength and help you to soar above life's storms on eagle's wings.

Loving You,

Your God of Wisdom

Psalm 46:10; Isaiah 40:31; 43:1–2; James 3:17

WISDOM'S WHISPERS

By Judy Carden

$\mathcal{E}$ight days into my month-long island retreat, a small residue of the drug I called *intensity* still trickled through my bloodstream. Nightmares disturbed my slumber and a low level of panic remained my constant companion. Figuring the pain would go away with time I waited and prayed that a month of island living would help me recover from an overdose of intensity.

Intensity is the drug of movers and shakers—the ruler of those who travel through life in the fast lane. In June of 1998, intensity, that false agent of the urgent, had temporarily seized my soul. I had done a poor job of prioritizing—putting work (yes, even inspirational writing!) before God and family. Finally, I was paying the price that women who do too much always pay: emotional and spiritual exhaustion.

"I really had myself convinced that all the worthy ventures I was doing were for the honor and glory of God," I shared with a friend during an early morning bike ride.

"Yeah, it's funny how we tell ourselves that, and for a time we believe it. But eventually, if we're not careful, God and family tumble to the bottom of the order, and we realize that we have been seduced by the world's artificial standard of what makes a successful woman."

That night as I lay on the beach under a star-studded sky, listening as soft waves washed tiny shells ashore, I thought, *How many times has God tried to whisper my name only to be drowned out by the hustle and bustle of my overcommitted life? And how often must I replay the voices of my family saying that they miss me before I change my ways?*

Late that night as I lay in bed, I heard the soft, still, voice of God nudge my heart: *Be still and know that I am God.* Only this time I listened—and changed. Today the intensity and anxiety return only when I fail to remember that God and family come first. When that happens, the gentle whisper of a loving Father reminds me again: *Be still and know that I am God.*

If not for the soft, still urgings of a

loving God, we might spend a lifetime

racing through life in the fast lane—

the wrong lane—missing what is

really most important to the true

meaning of happiness. How many

times has God tried to call our name,

only to be drowned out by the sounds

of fast-lane traffic?

You are the work of My hand. I created male and female, blessing both. Whatever you do, work at it with all your heart like you're working for Me, not for men. Surely, I'll individually reward each one of you according to what you've contributed.

Blessings,
Your Creator

Isaiah 64:8; Genesis 5:2; Colossians 3:23–24; Psalm 62:12

WOMEN WORKING

By Susan Duke

"Men have so much freedom!" I told my friend Bettie, during a discussion about the differences between men and women.

"Like what?" she asked.

"Well, they don't have to wear makeup. Their idea of a bad hair day means it's time for a haircut, and they shop the very day *of* birthdays and holidays. Getting ready to go somewhere takes me an hour, but my husband jumps in the shower, gets dressed, and is dangling the car keys in twenty minutes flat. He doesn't understand why a phone call to check on my mom takes thirty minutes. He makes a five-minute call to his dad and says he's found out everything he needs to know. He also tells me I have a Wal-Mart ministry because women I've never met tell me their life stories in the checkout lines."

"Well, I have to admit," Bettie said, "you don't catch many guys chatting in checkout lines. And, think about it . . . have you ever seen one man at a restaurant table ask another if he'd like to accompany him to the bathroom? We think nothing of it!"

"Maybe it's the Venus and Mars thing," I replied. "Have you

ever seen a man *swoon* over anything? Remember the day you found those great shoes on sale and got so excited people swarmed around to check out the bargains? When is the last time you saw a man displaying raw unbridled emotions over a sale? I'd fall over if I ever heard a man say, 'Wow! I'm soooo glad I found this fantastic sale table!'"

"I read somewhere that because men have fewer brain cells than women, they think more analytically with their left brain," Bettie said. "Maybe that's why they carry one hanger bag for a weeklong trip, while we take several suitcases."

"Actually, I think there's really only one thing between men and women I consider unfair treatment," I said seriously. "What's that?" Bettie asked.

"Those road construction signs—the big orange "Men Working" ones. Why don't *we* get to display big orange signs in our driveway while we're cleaning house that say, "Women Working"?

"Hey, chalk it up as a *man thing*! They need more recognition," Bettie said jokingly. "Must be those missing brain cells!"

The distinctions between men and women are by God's

design. He has created us emotionally, mentally, and

spiritually to complement one another and joyfully

celebrate the difference.

OTHER BOOKS BY STARBURST PUBLISHERS®

God Things Come in Small Packages for Women: Celebrating the Unique Gifts of Women
LeAnn Weiss, Susan Duke, and Judy Carden
Women will experience God's love like never before through powerfully translated Scripture, true stories, and reflections that celebrate the unique character of women. A new release from the elegant *God Things Come in Small Packages* series that combines the beauty of gift books with the depth of devotionals. Includes reflective meditation, narrative vignettes detailing powerful moments of revelation, and encouraging Scripture passages presented as letters from God.
(hard cover) ISBN 1892016354 $12.95

God Things Come in Small Packages for Friends: Exploring the Freedom of Friendship
LeAnn Weiss, Susan Duke, and Judy Carden
A heartwarming combination of true stories, paraphrased Scripture, and reflections that celebrate the simple yet cherished blessings shared between true friends. A new release from the elegant *God Things Come in Small Packages* series that combines the beauty of gift books with the depth of devotionals. Includes reflective meditation, narrative vignettes detailing powerful moments of revelation, and encouraging Scripture passages presented as letters to a friend.
(hard cover) ISBN 1892016346 $12.95

God Things Come in Small Packages for Moms: Rejoicing in the Simple Pleasures of Motherhood
Susan Duke, LeAnn Weiss, Caron Loveless, and Judy Carden
The "small" treasures God plants in a mom's day shine in this delightful book. Savor priceless stories, which encourage you to value treasures like a shapeless, ceramic bowl presented with a toothy grin; a child's hand clinging to yours on a crowded bus; or a handful of wildflowers presented on a hectic day. Each story combines personalized Scripture with heartwarming vignettes and inspiring reflections.
(hard cover) ISBN 189201629X $12.95

God Things Come in Small Packages: Celebrating the Little Things in Life
Susan Duke, LeAnn Weiss, Caron Loveless, and Judy Carden
Enjoy touching reminders of God's simple yet generous gifts to brighten our days and gladden our hearts! Treasures like a sunset over a vast, sparkling ocean; a child's trust; or the crystalline dew on a spider's web come to life in this elegant compilation. Such occasions should be celebrated as if gift wrapped from God; they're his hallmarks! Personalized Scripture is artfully combined with compelling stories and reflections.
(hard cover) ISBN 1892016281 $12.95

Purchasing Information
www.starburstpublishers.com

Books are available from your favorite bookstore, either from current stock or special order: use title, author, and ISBN. If unable to purchase from a bookstore, you may order direct from STARBURST PUBLISHERS. When ordering please enclose full payment plus shipping and handling as follows:

Post Office (4th class)
$3.00 with purchase of up to $20.00
$4.00 ($20.01–$50.00)
5% of purchase price for purchases of $50.01 and up

Canada
$5.00 (up to $35.00)
15% ($35.01 and up)

United Parcel Service (UPS)
$4.50 (up to $20.00)
$6.00 ($20.01–$50.00)
7% ($50.01 and up)

Overseas
$5.00 (up to $25.00)
20% ($25.01 and up)

Payment in U.S. funds only. Please allow two to four weeks minimum for delivery by USPS (longer for overseas and Canada). Allow two to seven working days for delivery by UPS. Make checks payable to and mail to: Starburst Publishers®, P.O. Box 4123, Lancaster, PA 17604. Credit card orders may be placed by calling 1-800-441-1456, Mon–Fri, 8:30 A.M. to 5:30 P.M. Eastern Standard Time. Prices are subject to change without notice. Catalogs are available for a 9 x 12 self-addressed envelope with four first-class stamps.